LA VIE EN ROSE
The Little Book of Joy

D0031978

Dominique Glocheux

Translated from French by Elisabeth Griffart-Meissner

CELESTIALARTS

Berkeley • Toronto

A Kirsty Melville Book

CELESTIALARTS
P.O. Box 7123
Berkeley, CA 94707
www.tenspeed.com

Interior and cover design by Larissa Pickens
Translated to English by Elisabeth Griffart-Meissner
Cover art by Jean-Pierre Desclozeaux

Distributed in Australia by Simon and Schuster Australia, in Canada by Ten Speed Press Canada,
in New Zealand by Southern Publishers Group, in South Africa by Real Books,
in Southeast Asia by Berkeley Books, and in the United Kingdom and Europe by
Airlift Books.

Library of Congress Cataloging-in-Publication Data
Glocheux, Dominique.
   [Vie en rose. English]
   La vie en rose : the little book of joy / Dominique Glocheux ;
translated from French by Elisabeth Griffart-Meissner.
      p. cm.
   ISBN 1-58761-111-2
   1. Joy—Miscellanea. 2. Happiness—Miscellanea.   I. Title.
   BF575.H27 G5813 2001
   131—dc21
                                    2001003818

Printed in Canada

1 2 3 4 5 — 05 04 03 02 01

To Aude Berlin, my little love who already belongs to the "Butterfly Generation," to my parents, because they have understood it all before me.

Merci à Françoise & Alexandra for flawless friendship.

Thanks to Fionna, Island, Jennifer, Laura, Liam, Margaux, M.B., Nikita & Tïuraï, for all the love and care you give me.

Merci à Calypso, Elisa, Gaby, Gaëlle, Jocelyne, Marine, Mylène & Zine, mes muses XXL, à Muriel & Alain Bosetti, à Laurence, Laurent & Fanny, à Christian Imniac, à Michaël Williams, à Thierry, à Claude & Morgane.

"All that is not given is lost."—Indian saying

"Happiness goes toward the ones who know how to laugh."
    —Japanese saying

"I have the simplest of taste, I'm only satisfied with the best."
    —Oscar Wilde

"I'll be only satisfied with happiness." ⤳

"Love to all of you…" ⤳

PREFACE

You only live once. There are no dress rehearsals in life, and you'll never have another chance to live present or future moments again—so why not see life in the pink? We can all benefit from living life to its fullest and appreciating each precious moment, and you don't need to have a black belt in the *Kama-sutra* or to alter your consciousness to do so! Often the simplest ideas are the most powerful. Dream of placing angel wings on your back and soaring to the top of each experience, leaving all your worries behind. Aim for serenity and bliss.

Herewith, I lend you my wings to use as you desire. But know that ultimately, the only wings that will ever truly lead you to happiness are the ones that develop in your own mind. I know this is true based on my own personal experience. Years ago I was struck by a taxi while walking down the street. Every bone in my body was broken, and I couldn't move in the slightest. Pinned down to my bed like a butterfly in a collection, my mind was full of black butterflies. Then after several months had passed, the first pink butterfly emerged—then another, and another, and another…

Read my "butterflies" and incorporate their suggestions into your life, then discover your own butterflies, your own way. Let intuition be your guide. Allow your butterflies to multiply in your mind. Nurture them; let them elevate your spirit. In time you'll take off on your own. It's magical.

Up until the eighteenth century, morals came from "above." Society was respectful of sacred and intangible principles, which were chosen and dictated by religion. In short, values were imposed on the self from outer sources. With the progressive secularization of our society, most of these austere obligations were first disputed, then devalued. The public morals of yesterday are giving way to personal ones. As a result, today we find ourselves liberated from sheepish obedience to external forces. We have the fantastic freedom to choose for ourselves, within ourselves, our own values, morals, and lifestyles. Never before in history have people been as free. We simply have to look closely at how we choose to utilize our freedom.

We all can be regarded as morally hindered at one time or another, but what progress we have made so far! Even if we cannot yet claim victory, comforting signs of civility are visible. The popular surges toward justice, honesty, generosity, loyalty, and honor are all indications of positive individual growth. We aim to introduce modesty and gentleness in our human relationships, to renew our relationships with the community, and to ritualize a bond with good manners, propriety, politeness, and courtesy.

This personal, gentle revolution is possible, because signs of praise for slowing down in our day-to-day experiences (or even laziness!) are on the increase—praise for the search for meaning rather than performance, a search for unity, safe harbor, and harmony. Life is interesting because it has meaning, either the meaning that we find in it or that we give to it. And meaning comes about only from taking things slowly. It is essential to learn how to create peace and silence within ourselves, to listen to the whispers of our consciences, to listen to our hearts, to rediscover our roots. Take the time to understand people, places, and things, to assimilate any given situation, to give money its true value, and to assess the true price of life and the true value of simple things—of small things that make all the difference. Rediscover these small and buried treasures that fill life with wonder and make it enchanting. Take time to let your sensibility reveal itself entirely, time to follow your intuitions, to dawdle, wander, and play. Take time to dream of a Bliss Zeneration.

Marvel at your life, see your life in the pink, make your life full of enchantment. With this newly found worldview, you will be rolling out the pink carpet in front of you. Moreover, happiness is contagious. As soon as your happiness shines its first rays, your family and friends will also benefit from it. It's like showering rose petals on everyone with whom you come in contact.

Let this book grab your hand and take you on a stroll with yourself, enhancing the best of yourself. Open your heart's doors and your soul's windows, and let a good armful of fresh air plunge in. Awaken new ideas, feelings, sensations, and desires within yourself, those that were there all along, but perhaps simply dozing. Let them bloom.

Flesh out your ideas for projects, those images you have been thinking of but haven't yet formalized.

Of course, you may not agree with all 512 suggestions, and that's okay. Perhaps you'd like to add some suggestions of your own based on your personal experiences? If so, why not share them with others? The sequel is in the works, so write me at D. Glocheux, La Vie en Rose, 50 Avenue Foch, 75116 Paris. (This is the address where the magical "Pink Palace" used to stand—it's true!)

For now I want to wish you a bon voyage, a wonderful journey. I hope you enjoy engaging in the process of finding in yourself the resources and answers to questions you may have encountered and wondered about since birth: Who am I? Where do I come from? Where am I going? My suggestions are simply a vision and, if you choose, a path to follow. I believe we are on the eve of the most wonderful human transcendence ever: a universal fusion and reconciliation of all religions and philosophies. That would be some event!

While you are waiting for this new Golden Age (and retiring at twenty-one years old!), I suggest that you try to stir up the world, even if it's only a billionth of a millimeter! It's so simple. What if we help the world take one more step in that direction? What if we decide to actively participate in transforming the world gently, along with the life that goes with it. Together, let's initiate a new way of life, new values, and sincere human relationships—greater ones, stronger ones, and nicer ones. Make your relationships pink like happiness, free like butterflies.

What if we decide to have pink butterflies fill our minds?
What if we choose to be the first Butterfly Generation?

Maybe you've heard of the theory by the climatologist Edward Lorenz of deterministic chaos, made popular under the name "The Butterfly Effect." According to his theory, the flapping of a butterfly's wings in Brazil may trigger a cyclone at the other end of the earth. Imagine for a second the effect of tens, hundreds, thousands of butterflies! Pink, all of them pink…

I wish you all the best, beautiful butterfly, and above all, live well.

—Dominique Glocheux ☙☙

1✓ Think simple.

2✓ For one day, try to reason less, and to feel more.

3✓ Learn how to cook three simple recipes. Prepare them like a gourmet chef.

4✓ Believe in love at first sight.

5✓ If you've never experienced something, go ahead and try it.

6✓ Learn to say *no* more often.

7✓ Stamp your letters with collector's stamps.

8✓ Create a comfortable and cozy interior for your home.

9✓ Cuddle a baby in your arms—it feels so good.

10✓ Smile at all the faces that cross your path. Smile big.

11✓ Love a pet—they are so soft and affectionate. Surrender.

12✓ Revisit the places and memories of your childhood.

13✓ Say "I love you" and "I missed you" more often.

14✓ Donate blood.

15✓ Go on a relaxing getaway with someone you love. It's less expensive with a Saturday night stay.

16✓ Stretch out like a kitten in front of a warm, cozy fire.

17✓ Take a risk each day. Small ones are enough at first.

18✓ Learn how to enjoy silence.

19✓ Follow your intuition; it's often right.

20✓ Join a choir. To sing with others is pure joy.

21✓ Reread *The Little Prince* by Antoine de Saint-Exupéry.

22✓ Don't save time. Use it up thoroughly.

23✓ Learn how to iron a shirt.

24✓ Let yourself be led by the star deep in your heart.

25✓ Have friends who don't know one another meet at your place.

26✓ Watch the disappearing cosmos an hour before dawn with someone you love—magical.

27✓ When you are driving, let pedestrians cross at their own pace.

28✓ Do what you love most. Do it often. And find ways to get paid to do it.

29✓ Buy some Bazooka bubblegum. Blow big pink bubbles.

30✓ When you don't know where you are going on life's path, you can end up anywhere—or worse, nowhere. Choose *your* direction.

31✓ Pretend there's a blackout just to see what you and your love will be able to make of the total darkness.

32✓ Give away lots of presents. Even if only small ones.

33✓ Buy twenty-five gifts for grown-ups and kids: Whenever you get a chance, buy anything and everything that fancies you. Tuck the gifts away in a secret spot for when you're ready to give them away.

34✓ While your baby is still in the womb, tape-record the heartbeat.

35✓ When a child loses a tooth, send the tooth fairy. It's so comforting to find a coin underneath your pillow.

36✓ Be in bed by 9 P.M. once a week. If it's a Thursday night, you can dream about a glorious weekend.

37✓ Keep a book of etiquette at home. Sharpen your knowledge of the rules and their uses.

38✓ Go to the beach or the mountains for the weekend. When you return, it will feel as if you have been gone for a week.

39. Find three ideas to SIMPLIFY your life. Try thinking "Less is more."

40✓ Buy sexy lingerie for yourself or your love.

41✓ Among all your activities, prioritize the ones that can be useful to others.

42✓ Each day either walk one mile or exercise for twenty minutes: Working out is a good way to rid your life of stress or the blues.

43✓ Always keep a bottle of champagne in your refrigerator.

44✓ In public when you are surrounded by people, whisper in your love's ear that she or he makes you happy.

45✓ During the next twenty-four hours, start a chat with each person who meets your eyes.

46✓ Meditate on this: Behind every ending, there is a new beginning.

47✓ Indulge in a favorite pastime.

48✓ Slow down your pace.

49✓ Surround yourself with people who see the best in you and encourage you.

50✓ If you're feeling depressed, watch children play at a park. They will take your mind off things. Instantly, you'll think life is fine. What magic.

51✓ Dare yourself to say to someone, "Hold on a second. Let me see, you have an eyelash that is about to fall into your eye. Come closer." Then softly blow—especially if there's nothing there.

52✓ When you are dining with your partner, slip a love note underneath their plate.

53✓ Write down the memories you've made since meeting your love. When you get to the last page, give it to them.

54✓ Rent a scooter for the weekend.

55✓ For one day, try to be 10 times more polite and courteous than usual.

56✓ Review your day before going home. Then decide not to think about it until the next day. Little by little, your workplace worries will move out of your private life.

57✓ Wear something sexy underneath your formal attire.

58✓ Learn how to identify the most well-known stars in the sky.

59✓ Drive a tractor once in your life.

60✓ When arguing with your family and friends, let them win. Choose to be happy, rather than being right.

61✓ Have your best friends over for dinner—even if you're too busy to do so.

62✓ As soon as you have the space, set up a swing set.

63✓ Call people by their first names; hearing their own names is music to their ears.

64✓ Whenever you speak, speak louder.

65✓ Whenever you walk, walk faster.

66✓ Whenever you sing, sing with a stronger voice.

67✓ Learn how to identify fir, oak, elm, birch, and maple trees.

68✓ Give your next 5 minutes a spontaneous tone. Grab whatever is within reach, and act on the first idea that comes to mind.

69✓ Remember that 20 percent of the effort produces an average of 80 percent of the effect. Beyond that is simply a waste of time. Nevertheless, you'll never be able to see the difference. Do your best, but stop as soon as you have reached 80 percent of the expected result…

70✓ …and be wary of perfectionism. The last 20 percent of the effect requires 80 percent of the entire effort. Don't waste 80 percent of your time trying to polish 20 percent of your work. Measure your actions. Perfection is spelled out P-A-R-A-L-Y-S-I-S.

71✓ End all your personal correspondences with a nice postscript. Reading one can be very moving.

72✓ Give to yourself
before giving to
others. You will
have more to give.

73✓ Just before falling asleep, whisper in your love's ear, "I love you."

74✓ Head to the swimming pool during lunchtime.

75✓ Spend twenty dollars on all sorts of greeting cards, just to have them on hand before any occasion.

76✓ Learn how to milk a cow.

77✓ Climb to the top of a monument or mountain. From above, everything looks so spectacular.

78✓ Enjoy a shot of wheat grass juice. To your health!

79✓ Rent a metal detector. Go in search of buried treasure.

80✓ Surround yourself with friends who inspire and motivate you.

81✓ Before starting an important project, reflect on how you would proceed if you had nothing to lose. Take note carefully.

82✓ Take a child to the zoo to see the monkeys and hippopotamuses.

83✓ At each red light, give your loved one a kiss.

84✓ Make a list of things that life has already brought you.
Be grateful for them...

85✓ ...and make a list of things you still want. Close your
eyes and make a wish.

86✓ Avoid justifying your behavior or trying to prove yourself
to others.

87✓ In private, ask the chef to make a heart-shaped pizza,
and have it served to your love.

88✓ Listen to Brazilian music, and let yourself be seized by the rhythm of samba. Imagine yourself on Copacabana Beach in Rio. Just let go.

89✓ Always have exercise clothes handy.

90✓ Never start sentences with "I shouldn't say this, but...," Hold your tongue.

91✓ Dare yourself to say this to a stranger: "I'm so sorry to approach you like this, but a force stronger than me said I just *had* to talk to you."

92✓ Write poems—even if you can't find perfect rhymes.

93✓ At least once in your life, drink the milk of a fresh coconut.

94✓ Don't let the smallest doubt, worry, or fear paralyze you; take some risks. Statistics show that if you take risks, you will reach your goals more often.

95✓ Doing the right thing is worth a million times *more* than doing things in style. Be efficient, never efficacious.

96✓ Take a child by the hand. It's so comforting.

97✓ Grow flowers at home.

98✓ Don't miss an opportunity to go horseback riding, especially on a summer morning by the sea.

99✓ Always do things that "just feel right." Trust your luck and keep at it. Lady Luck loves persistence more than anything else.

100✓ Make up a recipe—from a banana cocktail to a vegetable casserole to homemade chocolate cake. Try anything. Name your creation after yourself, write the recipe on a card, and pass it on to your friends.

101✓ Carefully choose the person with whom you are going to live: No other decision is more important.

102✓ Always wrap your gifts with special paper and ribbon.

103✓ Cook with olive oil.

104✓ Avoid lending money to a friend; it is rarely a good solution. Moreover, you may end up losing that friend.

105✓ Rent in-line skates for the weekend.

106✓ Be your lover's best friend.

107✓ Don't see today as the continuation of yesterday or you will be prone to procrastination. Live each day independently from yesterday or tomorrow. Make the best of each day.

108✓ Learn how to identify barley, oat, wheat, and flax fields.

109✓ "No fortune is so harsh that with prudence a brave man cannot overcome it" (Virgil). Fortune favors the brave. Be bold.

110. Hang in there!
If you think you're on
the right track, don't
stop. Keep going.

111✓ Indulge in a full massage at a spa.

112✓ Be willing to say "I need help" more often.

113✓ End unsatisfactory relationships or activities.

114✓ Eliminate from your vocabulary "I have to" and "I should." You don't owe anything to anyone.

115✓ Take a long hike by the sea or in the woods with someone you love.

116✓ Be tender and romantic, terminally romantic.

117✓ If you have to get up in the middle of the night, enjoy the dark quietude for a moment before going back to sleep.

118✓ Don't blow out the candles on other people's birthday cakes.

119✓ Be more curious. Ask more questions.

120✓ Welcome your love home with a big bouquet of flowers, wearing nothing at all.

121✓ Come to trust others. Do it spontaneously. Just let go.

122✓ Celebrate every success, victory, pleasure, and other event. Even the smallest.

123✓ Become involved in the fight against AIDS and cancer.

124✓ Spend a while surfing the Internet; that's what it's there for.

125✓ Reread the first love letters you received.

126✓ It's 5 A.M.: Go see your town or city waking up.

127✓ Freeze a gift or a love note inside an ice cube. Let your loved one discover the surprise.

128✓ Never pretend to be something you're not.

129✓ Take advantage of end-of-the-season sales.

130✓ On a sunny summer afternoon, lie down on your back with your love in the grass, hay, or straw.

131✓ Memorize your three favorite quotations.

132✓ As long as it's not put in motion, even an ingenious idea has no value. Think less. Act more.

133✓ On the night before a workday, make breakfast and prepare your things.

134✓ Visit some historical places.

135✓ Laughter cures all of life's little boo-boos. Have a dose of it.

136✓ Find out what your love's favorites are: sport, color, perfume, flower, magazine, dessert, movie, song, and so forth.

137✓ Take yoga classes.

138✓ In the springtime pick a bunch of young dandelion greens from a pesticide-free field and make a salad. With shallots and hard-boiled eggs, it's delectable.

139✓ "Man has nothing better to do than trying to be in agreement with himself" (Freud). Try.

140✓ Believe in Santa Claus.

141✓ Don't take yourself too seriously.

142✓ Record all of your family's and friends' birthdays on a perpetual calendar. Celebrate them all.

143✓ Train yourself to choose and lead your thoughts, feelings, and actions.

144✓ Wait for your love after work. Surprises are delightful.

145✓ Concentrate when your heart beats with emotion or melts with pleasure. Enjoy these moments. Let pleasures penetrate you...

146✓ ...and don't think of what might happen. You could ruin the moment.

147✓ Learn how to change a tire, check the tire pressure, and check the oil.

148✓ Call your love in the middle of the day, just to say "I love you" very tenderly.

149✓ Look people in their eyes.

150✓ Set your watch eight minutes ahead.

151✓ Cut and paste together a collage that mimics the front page of your love's favorite newspaper. Personalize the text to send love messages.

152✓ Allow some time to yourself. Alone. Without being disturbed.

153✓ Hide a love note underneath your love's pillow.

154✓ Many people waste their lives by wanting to earn it. Just live it.

155✓ Don't be a gossip.

156✓ Three golden rules: Give priority to your problems. Consider them one by one. Concentrate.

157✓ *Concentrate* means to forget about everything else and involve yourself body and soul in one single thing at a time without interruption.

158✓ Buy a red clown nose.

159✓ Think about the Chinese saying, "One cannot walk and stare at the stars, when one has a stone in his shoe." Get rid of the small things that bother you, quickly.

160✓ Close your eyes while you savor tastes, smells, and sounds.

161✓ Ask your loved one to keep one evening free a month from now. For thirty days the mystery will be as good as the show itself.

162✓ Take chances.

Often. Again.

And again. And again.

And again. And again.

And again. And again.

And again. And again.

163✓ Rent a convertible for the weekend.

164✓ Say "Hello," "Please," "Sorry," and "Thank you" more often.

165✓ Be the first to clap after a show or a speech.

166✓ Have a barbecue with your closest friends.

167✓ Find a new nickname for your love. Use it often.

168✓ Subscribe to a monthly crossword puzzle magazine. Keep one in your bathroom with a pencil and an eraser.

169✓ Nourish your child's soul.

170✓ Give your love a calendar on which you have checked off all the days that you want to spend with your love. Check off all of them…

171✓ …and mark those days with golden heart-shaped stickers.

172✓ Find a new perfume that expresses yourself.

173✓ Bring your dreams to the surface, especially your childhood dreams. When we forget our dreams, we die.

174✓ Learn how to mentally erase bad memories.

175✓ Never refuse an opportunity to speak in public.

176✓ Create an oasis for yourself where you can "recharge your batteries," get in touch with yourself, and think over solutions.

177✓ Visit a rose garden when the roses are in bloom.

178✓ Give in to your emotions. Laugh hard or cry bitterly if you feel like it. Let yourself go.

179✓ Go to the country to pick wild strawberries, blackberries, or walnuts.

180✓ If you could do anything, how would you change your life? Come up with at least three ideas.

181✓ Never miss a New Year's Eve countdown.

182✓ Close your eyes and make a wish.

183✓ For your love, buy lingerie that you would like to see them in.

184✓ Don't miss the chance to indulge just because you want something even better.

185✓ Get the most powerful and fully equipped food processor you can find. Simplify your life.

186✓ Frequently say "It's so nice to see you again!"

187✓ Take life one day at a time.

188✓ Observe nature from a mountain peak. It's spectacular.

189✓ Make a list of your favorite things: books, magazines, sports, singers, restaurants, perfumes, colors, and so forth. Each time you read your list, decide which one is your favorite.

190✓ Have one goal in mind. Walk straight toward it, without hesitation. Each step will naturally follow the last.

191✓ Tell children you are proud of them and that they have made lots of progress.

192✓ Wash your loved one's hair.

193✓ Don't worry about things that are difficult to change. Do your best and forget about them.

194✓ Buy ten big photo albums without thinking about it, and fill them with your favorite photos.

195✓ Learn how to love yourself as you are—inside as well as outside.

196✓ Take a class in Zen practices.

197✓ At the end of the workday, go home wearing a costume.

198✓ Ask your grandparents to help you create your family tree.

199✓ Avoid starting over again from scratch. Find ways to recycle your previous attempts and successes.

200✓ Whenever you can, eat lunch on the grass.

201✓ "There is no propitious wind for the ones who don't know where they're going" (Seneca). Guide luck toward you.

202✓ Be spontaneous.

203✓ Close your eyes. See in your mind's eye the three most blissful moments of your life…

204✓ …and concentrate on each of your senses: sight, hearing, touch, taste, and smell. Remember exactly what you were feeling during these moments of intense happiness.

205✓ Find a friend or neighbor who has a piano. Enjoy making music, even if it's not perfect.

206✓ Learn three magic tricks.

207✓ Add some color to your wardrobe. Dare to wear pink. Guide joy toward you.

208✓ Never ask for a discount before first knowing the total amount of the bill.

209✓ Let your thoughts bring you freedom, not confinement.

210✓ Never harshly criticize your loved ones. You will hurt them and put them on the defensive.

211✓ Hold a kitten in your arms. Listen to it purr.

212✓ Enjoy a Popsicle on the beach in the summertime.
Just kick back and relax.

213✓ The next time you fly, ask to visit the cockpit.

214✓ Organize a surprise birthday party for your best friend.

215✓ Carry pictures of all your loved ones in your wallet.

216✓ Have at least one fantasy, even if it's a little crazy.

217✓ Buy more fruits and vegetables.

218✓ Enroll in an art class. Try drawing, painting, sculpture…

219✓ …and take a dance class. Learn salsa and swing.

220✓ Give generous tips. Include a lottery ticket sometimes.

221✓ As often as possible, try to be with the right person, at the right place, at the right time.

222✓ Find new activities that will raise your adrenaline level.

223✓ Kiss each and every square inch of your lover's body. Make it last.

224✓ Get catalogs from at least three different travel agencies.

225✓ Learn how to water-ski. Build up to riding on one ski.

226✓ Please others for pleasure, not because you have to or because you want to be loved.

227✓ Slow down. Tell yourself, "I take the time to enjoy life." And take your time. Let yourself live.

228✓ Tell someone right away what bothers you. Don't wait for them to guess.

229✓ Don't compare yourself to others.

230✓ When people eat at a beautifully decorated table, everything acquires a special taste. Be sure to care for appearances.

231✓ Learn how to jump rope.

232✓ *Carpe diem.*
Seize the day,
here and now.
You'll never be able
to go back in time.
Enjoy each and
every moment.

233✓ Hug your loved ones—especially for no apparent reason.

234✓ Be generous.

235✓ Make a list of New Year's resolutions. Write them down. Try to hold to them for twenty-one days. After that you will have succeeded in carrying them out.

236✓ Say "Hello" to strangers as often as possible.

237✓ Pick up your love at the airport or the train station, no matter the day or time.

238✓ Decide that you'll never be jealous again. Not only it does change your life, but it can also be fun. Generally, others will become jealous of you.

239✓ Never wait for inspiration or energy. Dash to work. Go ahead even if it looks bad. Inspiration and energy will show up eventually.

240✓ Learn to juggle with two and then three balls.

241✓ Organize a fishing trip with your friends.

242✓ Bring flowers home at least once a week.

243✓ Go on a picnic with your love: by the seaside, on top of a lighthouse, or in the snow.

244✓ Take risks. To succeed, you have to increase your personal failure rate.

245✓ When greeting someone, take the time to shake their hand.

246✓ Stretch while breathing in deeply. Favor abdominal breathing; it's more regenerating.

247✓ Be good to yourself. Indulge.

248✓ Learn how to replace a light switch or fix a plug.

249✓ Encourage people to talk about themselves and their interests. You will be amazed by what you can learn.

250✓ Make more decisions, clear-cut decisions. And make a point to avoid going back on them.

251✓ Give more kisses and hugs—without any special reason.

252✓ Scratch a loved one's back…

253✓ …and ask them to do the same for you.

254✓ If you only had one year to live, what aspects of your life would you change? Come up with three ideas. Make the changes within six months.

255✓ If you were going to die tomorrow, what would you do with your last moments? Do those things within twenty-four hours.

256✓ Give yourself the right to express your feelings and feel vulnerable. Show yourself to the world. Be open.

257✓ Read stories to children.

258✓ Take a ginseng treatment.

259✓ Memorize one monologue of a character from classical theater.

260✓ Be yourself. Act by thinking on your own, instead of doing what you think people expect you to do.

261✓ Go with your loved ones to watch the sun set, the moon rise, and the stars appear. Make a wish together.

262✓ Play with your appearance: change your hairstyle, your hair color, your glasses, your makeup, your watch, and so forth.

263✓ File and organize press clippings that inspire you.

264✓ Visit a tropical fish aquarium. Take in the glorious colors.

265✓ Dedicate your time to the essential; tear yourself away from the rest. What is not essential is useless.

266✓ Rent a karaoke machine for a birthday party.

267✓ Trust your common sense.

268✓ Resist the temptation to rekindle a relationship that already ended badly.

269✓ Never try to be perfect. Never.

270✓ Create opportunities to make original wishes with a loved one.

271✓ Hold hands with your love, and jump forward together while making a wish.

272✓ Write some love notes. Hide them in ten different spots. What surprise and joy you'll bring when your love finds them.

273✓ Take the fliers that people are handing out on the street. They are paid to do this job.

274✓ Once in your life, take a ride on a camel or an elephant.

275✓ Are things getting mixed up in your head? Stop and take a moment to clear your mind. Straighten things up.

276✓ Open a fancy bottle of wine.

277✓ Buy 5 spiral notebooks to take note of your ideas whenever one comes to you.

278✓ Try to avoid buying things that imply "status symbol."

279✓ Give priority to projects and actions that favor your inner balance and peace.

280✓ Learn how to sew a button on a shirt.

281✓ Jump like a kangaroo or walk like a monkey just to make children laugh.

282✓ Dare to ask for the moon. You'll get more positive answers than you might expect.

283✓ Learn how to say "I love you" in Italian, Hebrew, Greek, Japanese, Arabic, Chinese, Russian, Swedish, Spanish, and French...

284✓ ...(Ti amo, ani ohev otar, s'agapo, ai shite imassu, bahibak, wo ai nei, ya liubliu tiebia, jag alskar dig, te quiero, and je t'aime.)

285✓ Visit the lavender fields of Provence, France. There's nothing like them.

286✓ Learn how to whistle.

287✓ Take classes with your love: archaeology, modern art, wine tasting, climbing—whatever you want. Just take them together.

288✓ Have a hundred fewer ideas or intentions, but act more often. Put action to work. Your actions are a thousand times more efficient than anything of which you can dream.

289✓ Avoid like the plague those who are always worrying or suffering just to feel alive.

290✓ Rock yourself in a rocking chair, a hammock, or wherever you want. Rock yourself. Slowly.

291✓ Be your own best friend.

292✓ Learn how to delegate more often. Succeeding by helping others succeed is the secret of success.

293✓ Don't waste even a second thinking about your enemies.

294✓ Create a "chain" linking together all of your efforts, each one giving support, rhythm, impulsion, energy, and strength to the next.

295✓ Climb a tree to pick cherries or plums, just like when you were ten years old.

296✓ Lie down by a crackling fire. Let yourself be mesmerized by the flames. Throw a dash of coarse salt into the fire to color the flames green.

297✓ Free your mind: Write down the most cumbersome and smallest things, and then forget about them.

298✓ Never give someone a book without writing a little note on the inside cover.

299✓ Make a wish for a loved one.

300✓ Wear your love's T-shirt after they have worn it.

301✓ Think **BIG**.
Life is like a mirror:
It will bring just
as much as you
expect from it.

302✓ During a snowstorm, sip a glass of hot wine flavored with cinnamon.

303✓ Attach small gifts to a bunch of helium balloons, and leave them in a room for someone to discover.

304✓ "Eighty percent of success is showing up" (Woody Allen). This first step is enough. Go ahead.

305✓ Create an annual party on the same date to gather all your friends. For example, the last Sunday of March.

306✓ Tickle your loved ones.

307✓ Have at least one sentimental movie such as *Pretty Woman* or *Sabrina* in your video library. Watch it when you're feeling tender.

308✓ If you choose a job you love, or if you manage to swap the tasks you don't like with those you like, you won't actually ever have to do any real work in your life. Stop working.

309✓ Respect your principles.

310✓ Videotape television. You cut the time spent watching TV by 50 percent. The quality of the programs increases 500 percent. All thanks to the VCR.

311✓ Dry your love with a warm towel from the dryer.
Very slowly.

312✓ Welcome each new morning with love, trust, and peace.

313✓ Listen to soft music.

314✓ Come up with three ideas to make your surroundings better.

315✓ Sing for no apparent reason. At the top of your voice or
softly. It's nicer with children around.

316✓ Measure your love's body: neck, chest, arm, hand, fingers, hips, thigh, calf, foot, and so forth—all of it.

317✓ Don't criticize a gift that somebody just gave you.

318✓ Stay away from people who belittle you or suck up your energy.

319✓ If you lack time three days in a row, allow yourself one hour to reorganize your priorities. Postpone or delay whatever is not essential.

320✓ Take a hot bath with bath salts.

321✓ Plant a tree for each important event, such as a fruit tree for a birthday or an oak tree for a birth.

322✓ Before planning an exotic trip, remind yourself of how beautiful your own country is.

323✓ Give your love a bag of gifts that are inspired by each letter of your love's name…

324✓ …and add some extras to it: confetti, tiny hearts, perfume, a photo collage, sand, a lock of hair, and so forth.

325✓ If you have neighbors that are happy with their plumber, their dentist, or their baby-sitter, ask them for their phone numbers right away.

326✓ Realize that you own your time and that you can make whatever you want of it with total freedom.

327✓ If you are taking a trip via airplane, plan on bringing a neck pillow and earplugs.

328✓ Take your love to the best gourmet restaurant around.

329✓ Take advantage of life. Wake up earlier in the morning more often.

330✓ Foresee your progress: What you'll become is more important than what you are.

331✓ Participate in a team sport, even if it's not on a regular basis.

332✓ Prioritize matters that are important to you. Other matters can always wait.

333✓ Be excessive. If your love likes chocolate, give them a five-pound bar.

334✓ Clean up your mind. A clear mind is like an open door to happiness.

335✓ Take the opportunity to attend an outdoor concert.

336✓ Get rid of all the austere and mundane parts of your life. Exterminate them sys-tem-at-i-cal-ly.

337✓ Tell your love why you love him or her. Start by giving the ten best reasons.

338✓ Search a grassy field for a four-leaf clover.

339✓ Break your long-term goals into subgoals. Be precise, clear, and make sure to have numbers and dates. Have ten goals maximum in all.

340✓ Draft a calendar with precise deadlines for each subgoal.

341✓ Be able to explain your goals, subgoals, deadlines, and the links between them to anybody who might ask about them.

342✓ Reread your list often. Memorize the order of your subgoals. Let yourself be led in the right direction.

343✓ Walk on cushions or a bunch of pillows. Recall childhood memories of fun and comfort.

344✓ Introduce yourself to complete strangers just to meet new people.

345✓ Walk through a revolving door with your love.

346✓ Permanently leave a good cookbook with color pictures open in your kitchen.

347✓ Often ask yourself; "What is the best possible use of my time at the moment?" Find the crème de la crème. Take action.

348✓ Lie down in a hammock. Look at the sky. Listen to the wind and the sound of the rustling leaves.

349✓ Organize bike rides with friends.

350✓ Draft and agree on two mini-contracts with yourself covering any goals you may have. See them to completion.

351✓ Make sure you won't be interrupted when you are concentrating. Your efficiency will be multiplied by three. Learn how to say no, and schedule appointments with others.

352✓ Help others. Spontaneously. For free.

353✓ Every day allow for ten minutes of exclusive attention to the love of your life.

354✓ Take up climbing or hiking with friends.

355✓ Decide that from now on, you will act only by choice and not by obligation or weakness.

356✓ Feed birds. Listen to them chirp. Watch them fly in the sky.

357✓ Pleasure comes first by waiting. Slow down. Be patient.

358✓ Keep a good book by your bedside.

359✓ Be silent. Reconnect with your inner self and deep wisdom.

360 Don't rely on your memory. Write down your ideas; otherwise, you can lose 80 percent of their power…

361✓ …and frequently review the best ideas you have written down just to expound on them, to nourish your creativity.

362✓ Celebrate full moon evenings with your love.

363✓ Play—with children, with friends, with whomever you want. Playing replenishes your fountain of youth.

364✓ Dance with a loved one every chance you get.

365✓ Every month buy a magazine or a book completely different from what you would normally buy.

366✓ Celebrate your first kiss, the first time you said, "I love you," the first time you made love. Create your own holidays, and make up new types of anniversaries.

367✓ Have coffee in a café at a five-star hotel. Make it last.

368 Have your worries undergo a laser treatment, not a scanner treatment.

369✓ On a summer morning, walk barefoot on a dewy lawn with your eyes closed. Enjoy.

370✓ Avoid watching the news on television. Read a newspaper instead; it allows you to be more selective.

371✓ Take sailing classes until you can go sailing on your own.

372✓ Don't say "See, I was right" or "I told you so." You won't gain anything from doing so.

373✓ Get down on your hands and knees and have a race. With whom? You decide.

374✓ Put your ideas in writing. They will become clearer and stronger, and it will be much easier to put action to your thoughts.

375✓ Do a bit of exercise every day. You'll be in better shape for "hanky-panky."

376✓ If you are in a hurry to be happy, never trust shortcuts. Ultimately, this will make you happier faster.

377✓ Take time to gaze at the next rainbow you see. Make a wish.

378✓ Smile at people—twice as often and twice as long. Smiling is irresistible, and it can change your life.

379✓ Many projects are never brought to light simply because starting dates or achievement goals were never set. Make a date.

380✓ Visit a natural history museum or a planetarium.

381✓ Never miss a chance to take a nap in a hammock.

382✓ Play with some clay.

383✓ Give your love an unexpected massage. Massage the scalp, hands, fingers, back, temples, forehead, feet, or toes.

384✓ Make lists. Two examples are a list for what you should pack in your suitcase or a list for what to put in the cart at the grocery store. With practice, fine-tune your lists. Nothing will be forgotten, and you'll be relieved of stress. You will also save a tremendous amount of time.

385✓ Never sacrifice your life for money or "happiness to come." You'll always be disappointed.

386✓ Try taking a different way home sometime.

387✓ Make a telepathic appointment with your love. At a certain time, stop everything and think only about each other.

388✓ Don't deprive yourself of yawning. Do it slowly, opening your mouth wide while stretching in all directions.

389✓ Resist the temptation to show that you're right. Let other people triumph for the sake of their vanity.

390✓ Several times a day, try hard to stop thinking or analyzing. Let your brain slide onto a wave of tranquility, floating in total freedom. Zen.

391✓ Have a giant poster made from the best picture of you and your love.

392✓ Learn how to tie a necktie.

393✓ If somebody asks you what you want, avoid saying "Whatever" or "Whatever you want." Make a choice.

394✓ Go parasailing at least once in your life.

395✓ Send a birthday card to your love every day for the thirty days preceding the big day.

396✓ Keep a nice lamp next to a really comfortable chair so you can read under heavenly conditions.

397✓ When you are concentrating, let the answering machine pick up your phone calls.

398✓ Before visiting an art gallery, eat lightly. You will feel your heart beat faster in front of the beauty.

399✓ Come up with three ideas that will offer more balance to your life.

400✓ Make peace with yourself.

401✓ Regularly visit places where there are people you'd like to meet.

402✓ Organize an afternoon of shopping with your friends.

403✓ Express your ideas with strength and conviction.

404✓ Make sure to learn a lesson from each slap in the face that life gives you. Otherwise, history is bound to repeat itself sooner or later.

405✓ Buy candies you used to eat as a child: Pez, Tootsie Rolls, Hershey's Kisses…eat them.

406✓ How do you visualize your dream vacation? Come up with three ideas and start packing.

407✓ Just before going to sleep, read to your love.

408✓ Fairies always want to make three wishes come true. Ask for a fourth one; you may get it too.

409✓ Accept the trouble of dealing with administrative tasks as if they were a civic duty. Then forget about them.

410✓ Go grocery shopping with your love.

411✓ Do some "mental cleaning." Get organized. By doing so you will magically clean up and organize your mind.

412✓ Take time to watch a bird builds its nest, a spider spin its web, and ants build their entire city.

413✓ Memorize the lyrics of your favorite song. In addition, memorize the lyrics of "New York, New York."

414✓ Read your love's favorite book.

415✓ Relish the simple joys of life.

416✓ Bring your love a bouquet of roses. Even if you don't know why, your love will.

417✓ Don't worry about the price tag of accessorizing your kitchen or bathroom with gorgeous amenities. These rooms are too important to cut corners on comfort. You can save on other things.

418✓ Avoid trouble. Doing so costs less and is easier than finding ways to get rid of it afterward.

419✓ Whatever the temperature is, at least dip your feet into the water whenever you go to the ocean. Jump in the waves. Breathe deeply.

420✓ Take one day of vacation per month. In the long run, you'll be just as productive but so much happier. Here's the way it works: Before taking a day off, schedule your time so you can finish things. When you get back, you'll be reenergized and work more efficiently.

421✓ Make fruit jam at least once in your life.

422✓ Spend some time in a bookstore.

423✓ Never miss a chance to go down a slide.

424✓ Take lots of pictures all the time. Don't wait to be on vacation or at a special event.

425✓ At least once in your life, take your love sledding or on a horse-drawn carriage.

426✓ Rent a telescope.

427✓ "Looking for remote happiness is done in vain if you neglect to cultivate it in yourself" (Jean-Jacques Rousseau). Meditate.

428✓ Lighten up in *all* the meanings of the phrase. Your life will be nicer, lighter, easier, and happier.

429✓ Memorize a simple melody on the piano.

430✓ Find just a little something that might embellish your love's day.

431✓ After a victory, let off some steam. Whether it's small or big, release yourself.

432✓ Never give financial advice.

433✓ Now and then decide to allow yourself to do nothing.

434✓ Ask your love what they consider erotic. You will learn a lot.

435✓ If something really catches your eye in a shop window, don't pass up the chance to buy it. You'll hardly regret a little purchase made in the heat of the moment. Don't confuse the price tag with value of things.

436✓ Do something unusual in your life. Think of the guy who dresses up like Santa Claus on every July 4.

437✓ Start a fire with wood that you have gathered yourself.

438✓ Visualize the scene of your dream coming true. Write down all the details you can see (where you are, the season, the time). Write down all that you're feeling, understanding, hearing.

439✓ "With constancy, one always ends up getting what one desires the most" (Napoleon). Be eager and constant.

440✓ Organize a romantic dinner at home. Include candles, decorations, gourmet dishes, soft music, fresh cut flowers, and thoughtful attentions.

441✓ When you procrastinate something important, look closely at why you may be afraid of doing it well.

442✓ Open your closet. Organize it and donate to charities all the things you haven't worn or used in two years.

443✓ Often tell children that you trust them completely and that you will love them forever.

444✓ Suggest that your love come to bed, and warm up their cold feet against your skin.

445✓ Have a résumé on hand at all times, ready to be mailed out.

446✓ Make it a point to go hang gliding, scuba diving, or skydiving at least once.

447✓ Get a VCR and an answering machine. You'll gain so much freedom.

448✓ Travel lightly.

449✓ In the spring when you see the first butterfly, the first bee, or the first swallow, make a wish.

450✓ Learn how to fly a kite.

451✓ Avoid pessimistic or frustrated people.

452✓ Face the ghosts inside you. Look them straight in the eyes. They'll end up vanishing by themselves.

453✓ Discover water sports: canoeing, white-water rafting, kayaking. Go to Colorado and do it.

454✓ "We have one tongue, two ears: the Ancients said it is why we should listen twice as much as we speak" (Zénon). Listen more carefully to others.

455✓ If you stumble, get up again immediately, without thinking. And if you happen to fall seven times, get up seven times.

456✓ As soon as you have room for a garden, plant some strawberries and a fruit tree.

457✓ Add beauty and sweetness to your life. Start with the easiest things: decorate, color, and embellish the place where you live.

458✓ Hang a wind chime by your back door. Listen to the wind make it sing.

459✓ Avoid guessing at other people's thoughts. Just ask them.

460✓ Perform magic tricks rather than feats of strength. Work less but in a better way.

461✓ Strengthen your strong points. Don't try to be in control of everything.

462✓ Each spring take a trip to Washington, D.C., to breathe under the blooming cherry blossom trees.

463✓ Live your life slowly: Wherever you want to go, you'll always end up there faster.

464✓ Don't worry about how much you're spending on a comfortable bed, nice sheets, and a gorgeous bedroom. You spend a third of your life there.

465✓ Give children and parents "their space." Let them do things their own way.

466✓ Learn how to identify a pheasant, a partridge, and a magpie.

467✓ Sleep under the stars with your love. Count the stars. Contemplate.

468✓ As your life ends, you'll forget about your mistakes; however, you will regret all the things you never dared to do. Be daring.

469✓ When buying comforters, pillows, and bolsters, try goose down.

470✓ Review your priorities: Start with what you really like, the items to which you're ready to give 120 percent of yourself. The rest will all fall into place sooner or later.

471✓ Take your love to the theater on the opening day of a new movie featuring his or her favorite actor or director.

472✓ One single idea can change your life. Open your eyes and prick up your ears. It may appear any time, without making any noise or when you don't see it coming.

473✓ Don't listen to people who might say the contrary: Everybody loves sincere compliments, especially when they are made in public.

474✓ Give a copy of this book, with your own dedication, to all your loved ones.

475✓ Throw a party at your house for no reason. But come up with one in case anyone asks.

476✓ Pamper yourself.

477✓ Do even the smallest things in life with care and love.

478✓ Overestimate your commute by 10 percent, with a minimum of eight extra minutes.

479✓ Bring your love to a sporting goods store.

480✓ Give your children as much self-confidence as possible. There is no greater or more precious gift.

481✓ Leave a flower on your love's pillow to let them know you're in the mood for love.

482✓ Success attracts success. Initiate action.

483✓ Pleasure attracts pleasure. Initiate action.

484✓ Action dispels fear. Move. Don't wait, because you'll
      never be 100 percent ready anyway.

485✓ Create an opportunity to toast the person who shares
      your life.

486✓ Go out to dinner with your love wearing matching
      clothes.

487✓ Spontaneously trust a new face. Distrust sucks up too much time and energy.

488✓ Try to fast for thirty-six hours. Drink only clear water.

489✓ Take your time when you drive.

490✓ Charm your love each morning as if you need to reconquer them.

491✓ Hang out in a park. Feed the birds. Sit in front of a fountain or by a pond. Bask in the sun.

492✓ Before giving a speech, slip away and sit somewhere private. Sitting straight in a chair with your hands on your lap, jump up and then sit down again and again like a spring for five minutes. This is a definite way to get rid of the butterflies.

493✓ Around August 15th, try to count one hundred shooting stars in the sky.

494✓ Celebrate changing seasons with your love. Create rituals together: intimate ones, funny ones, special ones, anything you want.

495✓ Elevate your mind.

496✓ Dare to ask questions—no matter what the answer might be. What is an embarrassing moment in comparison to mental liberation?

497✓ Lend a helping hand to someone who will never know that you are responsible for it.

498✓ Keep a diary with all your progress, victories, and successes. Even the smallest ones. It's a delight just to reread them.

499✓ Congratulate and encourage people each day.

500✓ Your conscience
is whispering. Be
silent so you can
listen to it, and
follow its advice.
Your conscience is
always right.

501✓ Approach your love from behind. Give a big hug and become an integral part of your love. Then try walking together at the same pace. With a little practice, you'll be able to close your eyes and let yourself be led. This will lead to even more intense sensations. Breathe into your love's hair and the back of their neck.

502✓ Learn how to completely relax yourself, to steady your muscles: your face, neck, shoulders, chest, back, and stomach. Let your thoughts float like clouds, without trying to retain them.

503✓ Happiness is contagious. Surround yourself with happy people.

504✓ Get up earlier each Monday morning: Feel life, the city, the people who are waking up. Plan projects. Think about the good things that will happen to you this week.

505✓ Every summer stand underneath a lime tree that's in blossom and inhale deeply.

506✓ Constantly collect new markers in life, rituals that only belong to you: surprise parties, commemorative photographs, new whims, unusual objects, clear-cut decisions, souvenirs, an incomplete list of your favorite things, and so forth. You will give more meaning, prominence, and landmarks to your life, and you'll become an alchemist able to turn the ordinary into the wonderful.

507✓ Come up with a signal that means "I love you." From a distance or surrounded by people, I can wiggle my nose with my right forefinger, and my love knows what I'm saying.

508✓ Let people go ahead of you in traffic or in a line.

509✓ Learn how to play a musical instrument.

510✓ Whatever the project, begin with the means you already have, without any delay. Go ahead.

511✓ Trust luck.

512✓ Take life by the horns. Don't save the best for last. Do it now. Life is too short.